Madeleine Albright

my itty-bitty bio

Published in the United States of America by Cherry Lake Publishing
Ann Arbor, Michigan
www.cherrylakepublishing.com

Reading Adviser: Marla Conn, MS, Ed, Literacy specialist, Read-Ability, Inc.
Book Designer: Jennifer Wahi
Illustrator: Jeff Bane

Photo Credits: ©Thomas Depenbusch (Depi)/flickr, 5; Unknown Author/Wikimedia/Public Domain, 7; ©Capo Alonso/Shutterstock, 9; ©Wangkun Jia/Shutterstock, 11; ©Michael Geissinger, photographer/Library of Congress/ Reproduction No. LC-DIG-ppss-01014, 13; ©Northfoto/Shutterstock, 15; ©U.S. Department of State/flickr, 17, 22; ©Rena Schild/Shutterstock, 19, 23; ©LBJ Library/flickr, 21; Jeff Bane, cover, 1, 10, 14, 18

Library of Congress Cataloging-in-Publication Data

Names: Sarantou, Katlin, author. | Bane, Jeff, 1957- illustrator.
Title: Madeleine Albright / by Katlin Sarantou ; illustrated by Jeff Bane.
Description: Ann Arbor : Cherry Lake Publishing, 2019. | Series: My itty-bitty bio | Includes bibliographical references and index. | Audience: K-Grade 3.
Identifiers: LCCN 2019004200| ISBN 9781534147003 (hardcover) | ISBN 9781534148437 (pdf) | ISBN 9781534149861 (pbk.) | ISBN 9781534151291 (hosted ebook)
Subjects: LCSH: Albright, Madeleine Korbel--Juvenile literature. | Women cabinet officers--United States--Biography--Juvenile literature. | Cabinet officers--United States--Biography--Juvenile literature. | Statesmen--United States--Biography--Juvenile literature. | United States--Foreign relations--1989---Juvenile literature. | United States. Department of State--Biography--Juvenile literature. | United Nations--Officials and employees--Biography--Juvenile literature. | Ambassadors--United States--Biography--Juvenile literature.
Classification: LCC E840.8.A37 S27 2019 | DDC 327.730092 [B] --dc23
LC record available at https://lccn.loc.gov/2019004200

Printed in the United States of America
Corporate Graphics

table of contents

About the author: Katlin Sarantou grew up in the cornfields of Ohio. She enjoys reading and dreaming of faraway places.

About the illustrator: Jeff Bane and his two business partners own a studio along the American River in Folsom, California, home of the 1849 Gold Rush. When Jeff's not sketching or illustrating for clients, he's either swimming or kayaking in the river to relax.

I was born in the Czech Republic.

It was 1937.

Where were you born?

German troops came to my country.

We had to move.

My family moved to the United States. We were **refugees**.

I was 11.

I studied **politics** in school.

I studied women in politics.

What's something you are interested in?

I did important work in Washington, D.C.

I was an **ambassador**. I helped the **United Nations**.

In 1997, I became **secretary of state**.

I was the first woman in history to do this.

WE WANT
BACK HOME
TO KOSOVA
I ♥ KOSOVA
USA

I was awarded the Presidential Medal of Freedom.

It was for working toward world peace.

I helped make a space for women in politics.

I continue to **inspire** women to share their voice.

What would you like to ask me?

timeline

1997

1930

Born
1937

2012

2030

glossary & index

glossary

ambassador (am-BAS-uh-dur) the top person sent by a government to represent that country

inspire (in-SPIRE) to feel the desire to do something

politics (PAH-lih-tiks) having to do with government and laws

refugees (ref-yoo-JEEZ) people forced to leave their country to find safety

secretary of state (SEK-rih-ter-ee UHV STATE) the person responsible for relations with other countries

United Nations (yoo-NITE-id NAY-shuhnz) an organization of countries that works together toward world peace

index